Attention Management

90 Minute Guides

Michelle N. Halsey

Silver City Publications & Training, L.L.C.
P.O. Box 1914
Nampa, ID 83653
https://www.silvercitypublications.com/shop/

ISBN-10: 1-64004-006-4
ISBN-13: 978-1-64004-006-9

Contents

Chapter 1 – Attention Management

A distracted workforce is less than effective. Employees who do not pay attention to their work can waste valuable time and make careless mistakes. Attention management is a useful skill that allows managers to connect with their employees on an emotional level and motivate them to focus on their work and how to reach their personal and company goals.

At the end of this tutorial, participants should be able to:

• Define and understand attention management.

• Identify different types of attention.

• Create strategies for goals and SMART goals.

• Be familiar with methods that focus attention.

• Put an end to procrastination.

• Learn how to prioritize time.

Attention Management Assessment

Evaluate the attention management skills you already have along with the skills you need to develop. Understanding what skills you have and being able to communicate these skills clearly will increase your chances of being successful in your career.

Answer the questions quickly and honestly. Do not over think your answers. Use the assessment to gauge which topics demand your immediate attention.

1. I actively listen to both supervisors and employees.   1   2   3   4   5

2. I work efficiently and do not procrastinate.   1   2   3   4   5

3. I keep focused on positive things.   1   2   3   4   5

4. I think strategically about achieving goals.   1   2   3   4   5

5. I easily transition between tasks.   1   2   3   4   5

6. I manage my time well.   1   2   3   4   5

7. I make SMART Goals.   1   2   3   4   5

8. I am able to prioritize well.   1   2   3   4   5

9. I effectively motivate employees.   1   2   3   4   5

10. I understand and apply the 80/20 rule.   1   2   3   4   5

Chapter 2 – Introduction to Attention

Every company and every manager wants to increase productivity. Constant access to information and the expectations to do more with less is overwhelming the workforce. People are easily distracted at work. Attention management allows managers and employees to increase their productivity as well as their personal job satisfaction.

What Is Attention Management?

Attention management increases the ability to focus attention and can be done at the individual and organizational level. Managers are encouraged to deal with their own attention problems before trying to influence employees in their organization. In order to understand attention management, people must be aware of where they focus most of their attention. Most experts divide attention into four different areas or zones. While the names change, the ideas are all the same.

Four Areas of Attention:

- **Intentional:** When working intentionally, people plan strategically and prioritize their activities.

- **Responsive:** In this area people are responding to the world around them. They spend more time putting out fires than working intentionally.

- **Interrupted:** People spend too much time answering messages and handling situations that interrupt their work.

- **Unproductive:** This occurs when people waste time at work. Unless you are taking a scheduled break, checking Facebook and chatting is unproductive.

Stop Thinking and Pay Attention!

The advice "stop thinking" may seem counterintuitive to attention management. Many people, however, are over thinking everything and focused on the wrong ideas. When we constantly think we do not pay attention to what is really going on around us. Our feelings control how and what we think. If we think that something is boring, bad, or a waste of time, we tend to give it less attention. For example, people are less likely to pay attention during a meeting if they believe it will not be productive. The ability to pay attention allows people to better connect with the world around them, better process their emotions, and organize the way they process cognitively.

What Is Mushin?

Mushin is a Chinese term that loosely translates to "no mind." The concept is used in training for different martial arts. A better way to understand Mushin might be to call it pure mind. Mushin requires people to reach an absence of conscious thought and emotion, which better enables individuals to focus on a task. Meditation is used to reach Mushin and as a result, better intuitive skills.

What is Xin Yi (Heart Minded)?

Xin Yi is a centuries old martial arts used in China. While the fighting techniques may not be helpful when handling situations at the office, the strategies linking the mind and body are useful. Xin Yi involves the ideas of Six Harmonies that also appear in Kung Fu and other martial arts. The three internal harmonies connect the mind with will, energy, and power.

Internal Harmonies

- **XIn** and **Yi**: Connects the mind (Xin) with the heart or will (Yi).

- **Yi** and **Qi**: Connects the will (Yi) with natural energy (Qi).

- **Qi** and **Li**: Connects energy (Qi) with power (Li).

Reaching the internal harmonies is usually done through moving meditation that links the mind and body.

Chapter 3 – Types of Attention

There are different types of attention that we all use to function in everyday life. Different types of attention are required for different situations. When attempting to manage attention, whether personal or organizational, it is essential to understand the different types of attention and how each type functions.

Focused Attention

Focused attention is what most people would define as paying attention. This is the type of attention that concentrates on a single task and excludes everything else. This can be done while studying or working on a project. Focused attention is difficult to maintain because it is not a natural human state, and it operates on a physiological level. Constant focused attention actually makes people tired.

Sustained Attention

Sustained attention is the type of attention that people use to focus on a particular task that takes time. It is also called the attention span. For example, reading a book requires sustained attention. The brain uses sustained attention to process information and adapt to different situations. Problems with sustained attention occur when there are distractions that keep someone from completing the task at hand. Most people need to refocus and return to the task after 20 minutes. There are three stages of sustained attention.

Three Stages:

• Grab attention

• Keep attention

• End attention

In order to sustain attention, it is important to remove distractions and occasionally refocus.

Selective Attention

Selective attention is what people use when they pay attention to a single stimulus in a complex setting. Having a conversation in a crowded restaurant is an example of selective attention. It is not possible to pay attention to every stimulus that surrounds us. The ability to filter out background noise and focus on one object or message is essential when we are consistently bombarded with information. The drawback to selective attention occurs when people disregard what is happening around them.

Selective attention can be manipulated. Marketing experts, for example, attempt to link their advertising messages to their customers' interests. They do this with the hope of grabbing the selective attention of people.

Alternating Attention

Occasionally people need to perform two tasks that require different cognitive abilities at the same time. These situations require alternating attention. An example of this would be taking notes during a lecture. In order to use alternating attention, the mind needs to be flexible and move between one task and another seamlessly. Alternating attention means that the work on each task is quick and accurate as the brain transitions.

Attention CEO

CEOs guide the direction of their companies. The attention of a CEO will determine the attention management of an organization. CEOs must focus the attention of their employees in ways to drive business and move the company in the right direction. Modern CEOs are faced with the dilemma of attracting and keeping employee attention. Understanding the different types of attention and implementing attention management techniques will allow CEOs to motivate employees towards greater success. In order to accomplish this, CEOs must focus their expectations of internal and external attention.

- **Internal attention**: Paying attention to internal procedures.

- **External attention:** Focusing on objects outside the organization.

Attentional Blink

Attentional blink was first defined in the 1990s. Vision is a key part of attention. Rapid, serial visual presentations show that when people focus on two targets in succession in a visual series, they are likely to miss the second target. This occurs when the second target appears 200 to 500 milliseconds after the first target. Research shows that strong emotions related to the targets make them easier to locate. Meditation is also shown to reduce the errors associated with attentional blink.

Chapter 4 - Strategies for Goal Setting

Goals are continually linked to attention management. Success, on both a personal and professional level, demands effective goal setting. Goal setting, however, requires careful strategy and execution. Simply writing down a list of things to do is not goal setting. Goals need to be made on an emotional and intellectual level in order to be achieved successfully.

Listening to Your Emotions

People often fail to reach their goals because they ignore the emotional aspect of goal setting. Emotions affect every aspect of a person's life. They influence health and factor into how well people perform at work. Feelings towards goals determine whether or not they are achieved. Feelings of obligation will only motivate someone so far. Goals need to be based on personal vision in order to be effective.

Vision

Vision statements allow people to create goals that relate to their convictions and emotions.

- **Recognize your values**: Reflect on what you truly value and how these values will shape your future.

- **Consider your goals:** What do you want your life to be like in the future?

- **Write it down:** Draft a vision statement, and revisit occasionally to make any necessary adjustments.

Prioritizing

People often fail to achieve goals when the number of things they need to do overwhelms them. Goals must be prioritized. It is not possible to concentrate on every goal at once. They should be ranked in order of importance so that plans can be made accordingly. It is essential to have balanced goals that reflect all areas of life. Personal values and visions should be used to prioritize personal and professional goals.

Examples of Prioritizing

Goals	Priorities
Earn a promotion	B
Buy a house	C
Become a mentor	C
Coach my child's sports team	A
Stay healthy by exercising	A

Re-Gating

Sensory gating is the process that the brain uses to adjust to stimuli. There is a direct connection between the ability to filter out distracting stimuli and performance. Stress, anxiety, and depression can alter the chemistry of the brain and reduce the effectiveness of sensory gating. In order to prevent cognitive issues related to gating, it is important to try re-gating. Gating can be improved by using relaxation techniques that help the mind focus and filter out the distractions. Setting goals require focus and a calm atmosphere. Before setting goals, attempt to use relaxation techniques such as meditation to clear the mind of distractions.

Meditation

The brain travels through different patterns of brainwaves in sleeping and waking states. Meditation affects brain activity and allows users to control these patterns. EEG's show the changes that meditation brings to the brainwave patterns. Each brainwave is connected to specific activities such as sleep, attention, meditation, hypnosis, music, and relaxation. Different meditation techniques will have an impact on the different types of brainwaves. Understanding meditation demands an understanding of the five basic brainwaves.

Beta

Beta brainwaves signal wakefulness. They are associated with concentration and attentiveness. People use Beta brainwaves to solve problems, but they are also connected to feelings of trepidation and anxiety. Anyone who is awake is in Beta. Meditation slows Beta brainwaves and allows practitioners to focus on the other brainwaves.

Alpha

Alpha brainwaves are a sign of relaxed consciousness. Alpha waves are considered to be the brainwave of meditation. They promote creativity and are associated with pleasant feelings and tranquility. In this state, a person is awake but not intently focused. This is the ideal state for intuitive thinking.

Theta

Theta waves appear when someone is in a deep state of meditation, hypnotized, or in a light stage one sleep. At this stage a person is not fully aware of his or her surroundings. Theta waves are linked to dreams and short-term memory. Children naturally have more Theta waves than adults. Theta waves allow people to recall facts easily, which is sometimes why answers to questions seem to come while falling asleep.

Delta

Delta waves accompany deep sleep that is without dreams. This is the slowest brainwave pattern, moving at 1.5 to 4 cycles per second. Few people enter delta when they are meditating. Only experienced practitioners are able to reach delta waves and still remain awake.

Gamma

Gamma waves are the waves associated with the ability to connect and process information. They also improve memory and keep the senses sharp. People with high gamma brainwaves are known to be more compassionate and known to be happier or more content. They are often considered to be more intelligent than those with lower

levels of gamma waves. Meditation is known to increase the
frequency of gamma brainwaves in individuals.

Chapter 5 – Training Your Attention

There are different methods that allow people to train their attention. While some of the methods may seem counterintuitive to attention management, there are great benefits to practicing them. Visualization may seem like a waste of time that should be focused on work, but it is not. Each person is different, and it is important to find a method or combination of methods that work best for you.

Mushin

Mushin may be difficult to describe. It is translated as "no thought", "no fear", or "no mind." A martial arts technique, Mushin occurs when the conscious mind does not stand in the way of the body and instinct. Mushin occurs anytime that intuition takes over. There are no logical steps to Mushin, but there are exercises to increase the chances of reaching Mushin.

Exercise:

• Sit comfortably in a quiet room with no distractions.

• Focus on breathing. (There is no need to breathe in tandem; be natural.)

• Try to keep the mind blank, and consciously release each distracting thought as it comes.

Meditation

There are different types of meditation, but most are used to relax the body and calm or focus the mind. Common meditations include Mantra Meditation, Steady Gaze Meditation, Transcendental Meditation, and Chakra Meditation.

• Mantra Meditation repeats sounds or words.

• Steady Gaze Meditation involves visually focusing on an object.

• Transcendental Meditation is done sitting with eyes closed.

• Chakra Meditation uses focused breathing and mantra to explore the chakras.

Each person needs to discover his or her personal meditation style. For example, some people find mantras distracting and prefer steady gaze. Transcendental Meditation is the most popular in a business setting. Beginners, regardless of the style they choose, often benefit from guided meditation with an instructor.

Focus Execute

Attention management requires people to focus and execute. Failure is often caused by a fear of success. When the mind focuses on potential negative outcomes, it is impossible to execute a plan well. Rather than focusing on the potential failures, people need to concentrate on the benefits of a successful plan. Remaining positive will allow people to focus on their goals and execute their actions accordingly.

Visualization

Visualization is a habit of creating a mental picture of a goal and believing that it will happen. Successful people in every field use visualization techniques. The process of visualization may seem odd, but visualizing a goal allows the mind to accept it as a concrete possibility rather than a vague wish.

Steps:

- **Choose a goal**: Visualization needs to be specific. Pick an individual goal to visualize. It is easier to start small.

- **Relax**: Find a time and place to relax and focus on visualization techniques.

- **Visualize:** Picture the goal in detail, visualize it happening in the present. For example, many athletes visualize their performance before a game or competition.

- **Accept:** Believe that the goal will come true. Affirmations are useful tools to bring acceptance.

Chapter 6 – Attention Zones Model

There are four different attention zones: Reactive, Proactive, Distracted and Wasteful. These zones were introduced in an earlier module. The attention zone determines productivity as well as personal stress levels. Attention management allows people to move out of stressful or unproductive zones and manage their time wisely.

Reactive Zone

Many people, particularly managers, spend most of their time in the reactive zone. Those in the reactive zone spend their time putting out fires and handling urgent needs. The tasks are important, but they demand time that takes away from scheduled projects. An example would be finding someone to fill in for a sick employee. The task is important and demands immediate attention, but it does not help the manager meet any of his or her goals or deadlines. Occasionally, a crisis will need to be handled, but attending to one crisis after another should never be a way of life. In order for people to move out of the reactive zone and stay in the proactive zone, they need to address the time they spend in the distracted and wasteful zones.

Proactive Zone

The proactive zone is where everyone wants to work. People in this zone work strategically. They are able to plan and achieve goals. Spending time in the proactive zone reduces the amount of time that is spent in the reactive zone because contingency plans will be in place. The proactive zone maintains relationships, budgets, systems, and personal well-being. Review your goals and plan accordingly at the beginning of each week to improve performance in the proactive zone.

Distracted Zone

The distracted zone takes up far too much time. Things in this zone seem urgent, but they are not really important. The distracted zone occurs when other people monopolize your attention. Things like emails and phone calls fall under the distracted zone. Important time and energy is given to other people's priorities rather than personal goals.

Leaving the distracted zone:

- **Turn off email alert**: Emails do not always need to be answered immediately. Constant email alerts are distractions that take people out of the proactive zone.

- **Create a time-blocked schedule**: Schedule time to return phone calls and emails and build relationships. Work on projects during the time set aside for them, and do not allow yourself to become distracted by other people.

- **Set boundaries**: Stick to the schedule. Do not allow people to draw you away unless it is a **real** emergency. Be firm, and people will learn to respect your schedule.

Wasteful Zone

The wasteful zone is exactly what it sounds like, the zone where people waste time. Activities that waste time include checking personal email, looking at social media sites, online videos, and other activities that are not productive. It is important to note that people need to occasionally decompress. When time to relax and regroup is not included in a person's schedule, more time will be spent in the wasteful zone.

Leaving the wasteful zone:

- **Schedule personal time**: Take the time to relax, meditate, eat, and socialize. It is not possible to continually focus on a single task, so schedule breaks and take them. It will increase productivity and prevent the need for mind numbing activities.

- **Limit temptation**: Internet junkies should turn off their connection when they do not need the Internet, if possible. Turn off mobile devices when working, and indulge pastimes only when appropriate. Remind yourself that the wasteful zone keeps you out of the proactive zone and away from your goals

Chapter 7 – SMART Goals

The importance of goal setting has already been addressed. In order to achieve these goals, however, it is essential to create SMART goals. SMART goals guide people as they works towards an end. They eliminate confusion and increase satisfaction. While they are a staple in business settings, SMART goals are able to motivate personal and professional goals.

The Three P's

There are three P's to achieving goals. Approaching goals the wrong way will only end in failure. The three P's can help prevent people from becoming discouraged and motivate them to keep moving forward. When setting goals, make sure that they are positive, personal, and present.

- **Positive:** Goals should be written in a positive light. Rather than writing "stop wasting time", write, "become more productive."

- **Personal:** Goals need to connect on a personal and emotional level.

- **Present:** Similar to visualization, create goals that can be achieved immediately. For example, immediately stop surfing the Internet at work.

The SMART Way

Attention management is used to meet specific goals and objectives. Goals and objectives give participants motivation and a sense of direction. The goals and objectives of any strategy need to be SMART. SMART goals are particularly useful because they break long-term goals into short-term goals. For example, a long-term goal may be "become CEO", but a SMART goal would be "be promoted within a year."

- **Specific:** Goals should have specific directions. An example of a specific goal would be visualizing 10 minutes a day.

- **Measurable:** You should know when you reach your goals. For example, increasing productivity three percent is specific, and becoming more productive is not specific.

- **Attainable:** Goals, especially short-term goals, must be attainable. A goal to double your income in the next month is probably not attainable.

- **Relevant:** Goals need to be relevant to each situation. A goal to increase sales is not relevant to someone in production.

- **Timely:** Goals need specific timeframes. For example, spending less time in the reactive zone within three months is a timely goal.

Prioritizing

SMART goals, like every other goal, need prioritizing. Consider how SMART goals align with your personal vision and values. A goal that does not meet a personal need is less likely to be reached. Use the same criteria to rank SMART goals that you use to rank your general goals. Again, try to balance the goals between different areas of your life.

Goals	Priorities
Earn bonus in two months	B
Learn a new system in a week	C
Finish a project two days early	C
Create a schedule for the week	A
Exercise three times and week	A

Evaluating and Adapting

Once a SMART goal is created, it needs to be evaluated. Is it SMART? Does it follow the three P's? Is it a priority? Consider the steps that are necessary to reach the goal. Even if the goal is achievable, are you willing to do what is necessary to reach it? For example, if saving 100 dollars a month means never eating out, are you willing to give up the luxury? If not, adapt the goal to saving 50 dollars every month.

It is also important to review goals periodically. Circumstances change, and changes will affect goals. Re-evaluate and adapt goals to meet any new requirements or personal visions.

Keeping Yourself Focused

Staying focused is easier said than done. Even with SMART goals and schedules, there is always something trying to distract us. We can become overwhelmed by everything that we have to do. Looking at the big picture can be discouraging and cause us to lose heart. Fortunately, there are useful methods that help people stay focused.

The One Minute Rule

Everyone hates doing the little things. They seem unimportant, but when left to pile up, they can destroy focus and waste time. Did you ever let the sink pile up with dishes? How long did it take to do the pile of dishes? The one minute rule eliminates this type of situation; it reduces stress and creates focus.

The one minute rule advises people to complete any task that only takes a minute. Examples include filing a paper, putting office supplies away, or washing a dish. A minute does not really cut into your schedule, and it saves you the time in the long run. Filing a single paper every day takes a minute. Filing a month of papers will require much more time.

The Five Minute Rule

Schedules help people focus and manage their time better when they are done correctly. A common mistake that people make with schedules is making them too strict. It is not possible to plan the day down to the minute. When creating a schedule, follow the five minute rule. The five minute rule is simple: allow at least five minutes between tasks. A slight buffer will provide time to complete one task before transitioning to another.

What to Do When You Feel Overwhelmed

Everyone becomes overwhelmed. It is important, however, not to let your feelings control your actions. There are steps to take whenever you feel overwhelmed that will make it easier to regain focus.

Steps:

- **Stop**: Slow down before you panic and try to keep perspective. Take a moment to relax and think when you are overwhelmed.

- **Take Breaks**: Plan to take a five-minute break for every hour of work. Use the time to try relaxation techniques.

- **Break down tasks:** Break tasks into smaller steps.

- **Sleep:** Get enough rest to ensure you can think critically.

Chapter 8 – Procrastination

Everyone is guilty of procrastination from time to time. Procrastination is the enemy of productivity. When we procrastinate, we put off doing what we need to do. We usually procrastinate with leisure activities that gratify us for the moment but hurt our chances of long-term success. There are ways to fight off procrastination.

Why We Procrastinate

We usually do not mean to procrastinate. Sometimes a five minute break can lead to an hour long session of surfing the Internet. Each person procrastinates for different reasons. Identifying the reasons for procrastination will help people overcome it.

Reasons:

- **Stress**: Being stressed and exhausted triggers a fight or flight response. This reduces logical thinking and increases the chance of procrastination.

- **Fear**: Both fear of failure and fear of success result in procrastination.

- **Boredom**: Some people naturally delay gratification better than others. When we are bored, the desire for immediate gratification increases.

Nine Ways to Overcome Procrastination

Your ability to select your most important task at any given moment, and then to start on that task and get it done both quickly and well, will probably have greatest impact on your success than any other quality or skill you can develop! If you nurture the habit of setting clear priorities and getting important tasks quickly finished, the majority of your time management issues will simply fade away.

Here are some ways to get moving on those tough tasks.

- **DELETE IT.** What are the consequences of not doing the task at all? Consider the 80/20 rule; maybe it doesn't need to be done in the first place.

- **DELEGATE.** If the task is important, ask yourself if it's really something that you are responsible for doing in the first place. Know your job description and ask if the task is part of your responsibilities. Can the task be given to someone else?

- **DO IT NOW.** Postponing an important task that needs to be done only creates feelings of anxiety and stress. Do it as early in the day as you can.

- **ASK FOR ADVICE.** Asking for help from a trusted mentor, supervisor, coach, or expert can give you some great insight on where to start and the steps for completing a project.

- **CHOP IT UP.** Break large projects into milestones, and then into actionable steps. As Bob Proctor says, "Break it down into the ridiculous." Huge things don't look as big when you break it down as small as you can.

- **OBEY THE 15 MINUTE RULE.** To reduce the temptation of procrastination, each actionable step on a project should take no more than 15 minutes to complete.

- **HAVE CLEAR DEADLINES.** Assign yourself a deadline for projects and milestones and write it down in your day planner or calendar. Make your deadlines known to other people who will hold you accountable.

- **GIVE YOURSELF A REWARD.** Celebrate the completion of project milestones and reward yourself for getting projects done on time. It will provide positive reinforcement and motivate you toward your goals.

- **REMOVE DISTRACTIONS.** You need to establish a positive working environment that is conducive to getting your work done. Remove any distractions.

Eat That Frog

There is a saying of Mark Twain's that aptly defines ending procrastination.

If the first thing you do each morning is to eat a live frog, you can go through the day with the satisfaction of knowing that that is probably the worst thing that is going to happen to you all day long!

Your frog is the task that will have the greatest impact on achieving your goals, and the task that you are most likely to procrastinate starting.

Another version of this saying is, "If you have to eat two frogs, eat the ugliest one first!"

This is another way of saying that if you have two important tasks before you, start with the biggest, hardest, and most important task first. Discipline yourself to begin immediately and then to persist until the task is complete before you go on to something else. You must resist the temptation to start with the easier task. You must also continually remind yourself that one of the most important decisions you make each day is your choice of what you will do immediately and what you will do later, or postpone indefinitely.

Finally, "If you have to eat a live frog, it does not pay to sit and look at it for a very long time!"

The key to reaching high levels of performance and productivity is for you to develop the lifelong habit of tackling your major task first thing each morning. Don't spend excessive time planning what you will do. You must develop the routine of "eating your frog" before you do anything else and without taking too much time to think about it.

Successful, effective people are those who launch directly into their major tasks and then discipline themselves to work steadily and single-mindedly until those tasks are complete.

In the business world, you are paid and promoted for achieving specific, measurable results. You are paid for making a valuable contribution that is expected of you. But many employees confuse activity with accomplishment and this causes one of the biggest problems in organizations today, which is failure to execute.

Chapter 9 – Prioritizing Your Time

Successful attention management demands that you learn to prioritize your time. Establishing priorities shows you where to focus your energy. Priorities should be used to create goals and schedule your time. There are different tools available that will help you prioritize your time.

The 80/20 Rule

The 80 / 20 rule states that 80 percent of our success comes from only 20 percent of our actions. This means that it is necessary to focus on the 20 percent of our actions that are the most effective. Prioritize goals, and focus on the 20 percent of activities that actively move you towards those goals. Give most of your attention to this 20 percent.

The Urgent / Important Matrix

We are often trapped performing urgent tasks that are not important. The distracted zone is an example of tasks that are urgent but not important. They may be important to the people around you, but they do nothing to help you meet your own goals. Important tasks should take priority because they are focused on specific goals. The proactive zone is an example of important activities.

The Urgent/Important Matrix:

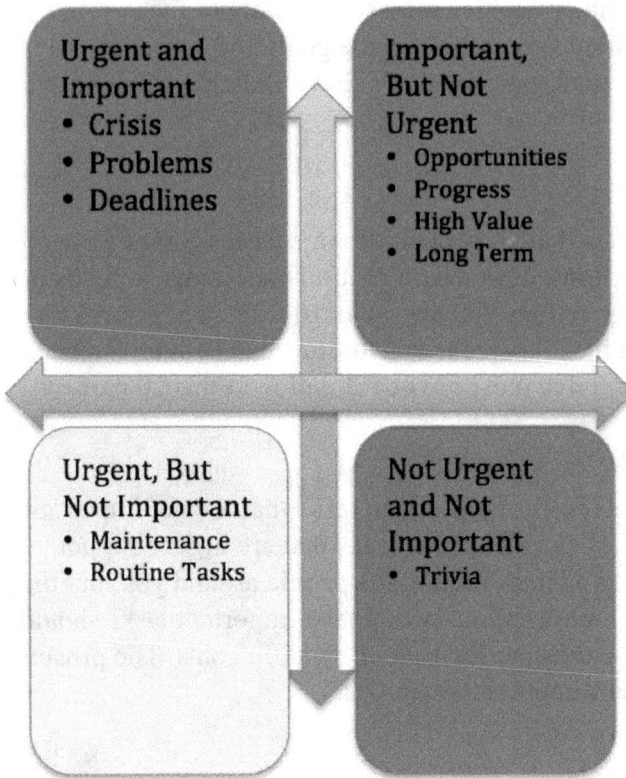

Urgent and Important	Important, But Not Urgent
• Crisis • Problems • Deadlines	• Opportunities • Progress • High Value • Long Term
Urgent, But Not Important • Maintenance • Routine Tasks	**Not Urgent and Not Important** • Trivia

- **URGENT AND IMPORTANT**: Activities in this area relate to dealing with critical issues as they arise and meeting significant commitments. *Perform these duties now.*

- **IMPORTANT, BUT NOT URGENT:** These success-oriented tasks are critical to achieving goals. *Plan to do these tasks next.*

- **URGENT, BUT NOT IMPORTANT:** These chores do not move you forward toward your own goals. Manage by delaying them, cutting them short and rejecting requests from others. *Postpone these chores.*

- **NOT URGENT AND NOT IMPORTANT:** These trivial interruptions are just a distraction, and should be avoided if possible. However, be careful not to mislabel things like time with family and recreational activities as not important. *Avoid these distractions altogether.*

Being Assertive

At times, requests from others may be important and need immediate attention. Often, however, these requests conflict with our values and take time away from working toward your goals. Even if it is something we would like to do but simply don't have the time for, it can be very difficult to say no. One approach in dealing with these types of interruptions is to use a Positive No, which comes in several forms.

- Say no, followed by an honest explanation, such as, "I am uncomfortable doing that because…"

- Say no and then briefly clarify your reasoning without making excuses. This helps the listener to better understand your position. Example: "I can't right now because I have another project that is due by 5 pm today."

- Say no, and then give an alternative. Example: "I don't have time today, but I could schedule it in for tomorrow morning."

- Empathetically repeat the request in your own words, and then say no. Example: "I understand that you need to have this paperwork filed immediately, but I will not be able to file it for you."

- Say yes, give your reasoning for not doing it, and provide an alternative solution. Example: "Yes, I would love to help you by filing this paperwork, but I do not have time until tomorrow morning."

- Provide an assertive refusal and repeat it no matter what the person says. This approach may be most appropriate with aggressive or manipulative people and can be an effective strategy to control your emotions. Example: "I understand how you feel, but I will not [or cannot]…" Remember to stay focused and not become sidetracked into responding to other issues.

Creating a Productivity Journal

Keeping track of how you spend your time and how productive you are will allow you to evaluate your priorities. A productivity journal is a useful tool that shows you where you spend your time and how effectively you are using it. A productivity journal is similar to a time log, and a spreadsheet can be used to create one. The journal needs to include three things:

- Activities

- Time spent on each activity

- Progress or outcome of the activity

The Glass Jar: Rocks, Pebbles, Sand and Water

The "rocks in a glass jar demonstration" is a familiar time management technique that is used to illustrate the importance of establishing priorities. A glass jar is filled with large rocks then pebbles. This is followed by sand and water. The purpose of the exercise is to teach participants that they need to put the large rocks in first or they will not fit later. The large rocks symbolize the priorities in our lives that are aligned with our values and goals.

Additional Titles

The 90 Minute Guide series of books covers a variety of general business skills and are intended to be completed in 90 minutes or less. It is an effective way for building your skill set and can be used to acquire professional development units needed by project managers and other industries to maintain their certification. For the availability of titles please see

https://www.silvercitypublications.com/shop/.

No. 1 - Appreciative Inquiry

No. 2 - Assertiveness and Self Control

No. 3 - Attention Management

No. 4 - Body Language Basics

No. 5 - Business Acumen

No. 6 - Business and Etiquette

No. 7 - Change Management

No. 8 - Coaching and Mentoring

No. 9 - Communications Strategies

No. 10 - Conflict Resolution

No. 11 - Creative Problem Solving

No. 12 - Delivering Constructive Criticism

No. 13 - Developing Creativity

No. 14 - Developing Emotional Intelligence

No. 15 - Developing Interpersonal Skills

No. 16 - Developing Social Intelligence

No. 17 - Employee Motivation

No. 18 - Facilitation Skills

No. 19 - Goal Setting and Getting Things Done

No. 20 - Knowledge Management Fundamentals

No. 21 - Leadership and Influence

No. 22 - Lean Process and Six Sigma Basics

No. 23 - Managing Anger

No. 24 - Meeting Management

No. 25 - Negotiation Skills

No. 26 - Networking Inside a Company

No. 27 - Networking Outside a Company

No. 28 - Office Politics for Managers

No. 29 - Organizational Skills

No. 30 - Performance Management

No. 31 - Presentation Skills

No. 32 - Public Speaking

No. 33 - Servant Leadership

www.ingramcontent.com/pod-product-compliance
Lightning Source LLC
Chambersburg PA
CBHW060706280326
41933CB00012B/2321